· 22184                          Jnf 599.5

DEMCO

# SAVING THE WHALE

First published in the
United States in 1987 by
Gloucester Press
387 Park Avenue South
New York, NY 10016

ISBN 0-531-17061-6

Library of Congress Catalog
Card Number: 87-80459

Printed in Belgium

Designed and produced by
Aladdin Books Ltd
70 Old Compton Street
London W1

Design      Rob Hillier
Editor      Denny Robson
Researcher  Cecilia Weston-Baker
Illustrator Ron Hayward Associates

The front cover photograph shows a dead sperm whale being winched to a factory in the Azores. The back cover photograph shows two right whales and their calf at the Peninsula Valdes in Argentina.

The author, Michael Bright, is a Senior Producer at the BBC's Natural History Unit, Bristol, UK. He is also the author of several books on Natural History.

# Contents

# SAVING THE WHALE

## Michael Bright

## Gloucester Press
New York : London : Toronto : Sydney

# Introduction

Whaling is an environmental issue that has touched the conscience of the world. Whales have been swimming in the world's oceans for over 50 million years. Yet the human race has taken only six centuries to bring many of the great whales to the edge of extinction. It is not, however, simply a case of there being fewer and fewer whales. There is a moral problem here too. Some whales and their smaller relatives, the dolphins, are among the most intelligent mammals on earth. So should they be considered a legitimate food resource?

Over recent years, world attention has focused on the plight of the whales. In 1986 a five year ban on commercial whaling was introduced; it is an international agreement reached by the member nations of the International Whaling Commission (IWC). Since the ban is voluntary there is room to "cheat," and the killing of whales continues. Many countries, including the USA, Canada, USSR, Norway, Denmark, Iceland and Japan, still support the often cruel slaughter, even though they officially observe the ban.

▽ A southern right whale leaps out of the water and crashes back in a mountain of spray. This is called "breaching." In this way a great whale can communicate with a distant one by the sound of a loud splash.

Some of these nations justify the killings by claiming they are part of aboriginal traditions. In other cases whaling is disguised as science.

In this book, we look at the killing of whales. Can their slaughter ever be justified or should the present ban be made permanent?

# Why kill whales?

Today whales are killed mainly for meat that is eaten in luxury restaurants and homes in Iceland, Norway and Japan. Over the years, however, whales have been killed to provide many products. Blubber used to be boiled down to make oil for oil-lamps or used in the production of margarines and soaps. The sieve-like plates in the mouths of baleen whales were used to stiffen corsets. Vitamin A was obtained from the liver and insulin from the pancreas. Oil from the head of the sperm whale was used to make smokeless candles, for the lubrication of fine machinery and in cosmetics. Now there are substitutes for all whale products. Vegetable oils, for example, are used in margarines and oil from the jojoba bean can replace sperm whale oil.

▽ The photograph (bottom left) shows a great whale hauled onto the deck of a whale factory ship. It is being hacked up before being "processed" into a variety of whale products. Meat from traditional Norwegian shore-based whaling reaches stalls in Bergen market, shown below.

6

The Japanese whalers place more importance on whale meat than on oil. Despite a superabundance worldwide of protein-rich foods, such as beef, poultry and dairy products, Japan would like to continue to consume whale meat. Japan is a country with many millions of people squeezed into a small living space and so there is limited land for agricultural expansion. Japan has a tradition of exploiting the sea as its main food source, and it sees whales as a legitimate part of that harvest. Indeed, the Japanese do not recognize that whaling is cruel. Most whale meat in Japan, however, is not really supplementing the diet of the average Japanese. It is a luxury food served at the most expensive restaurants.

"Japan cannot accept the argument that whaling is more cruel than the killing of other livestock."

Statement from the Japanese Embassy in London

Whale oils, particularly those extracted from sperm whales, used to be used in the manufacture of certain expensive lipsticks.

Today, synthetic oils have replaced whale oils, although in some cosmetics, natural oils from sharks are still used.

# Overfishing

Since its very beginning, the whaling industry has been guilty of overfishing. The whalers would hunt the whales from one part of the ocean and then move on to the next, until most of the whales in the world had been caught. The Basques, in the 14th century, were the first commercial whalers. They wiped out the right whales (they were the "right" or easiest whales to catch) in the Bay of Biscay. The British and the Dutch removed most of the whales from around Spitzbergen, and then moved on to Greenland and Newfoundland. When the Arctic was fished out, the whalers turned to the Antarctic.

▽ The photograph shows a row of whale corpses. Whales have always been caught in large numbers. At first whales were caught from small rowing boats and struck with hand-held harpoons. Whalers were towed around the oceans until their catch became exhausted. The more recent Antarctic whalers had fast steamships equipped with harpoon guns and were able to catch hundreds of whales each day.

In the Southern Ocean, the giant blue whales were the first targets of the modern whaling industry. They provided whalers with the highest rewards. One whale might yield up to 50 tons of oil. The largest taken was 33.6m (110 ft) long. In the early 1960s there were not enough blue whales to catch and the whalers turned to smaller whales. It was not, however, the disappearance of one stock of whales after another that gave rise to the first international agreements to conserve whales. It was a slump in the price of whale oil and the loss of profits that led to a restriction on catches.

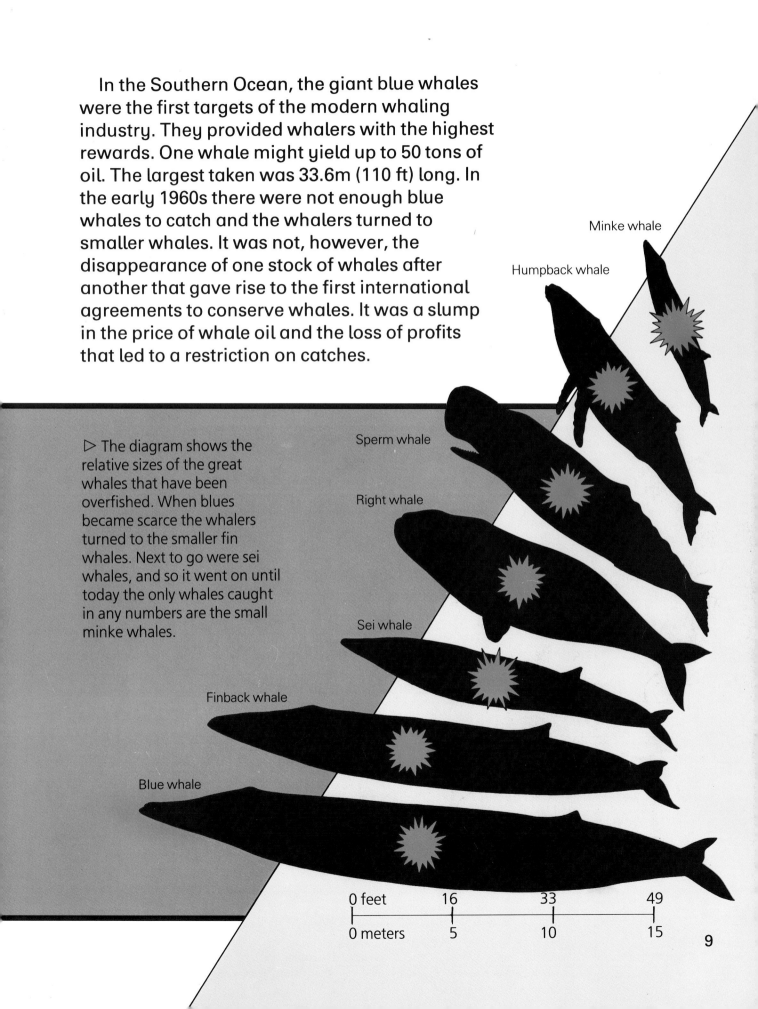

▷ The diagram shows the relative sizes of the great whales that have been overfished. When blues became scarce the whalers turned to the smaller fin whales. Next to go were sei whales, and so it went on until today the only whales caught in any numbers are the small minke whales.

Minke whale

Humpback whale

Sperm whale

Right whale

Sei whale

Finback whale

Blue whale

| 0 feet | 16 | 33 | 49 |
|---|---|---|---|
| 0 meters | 5 | 10 | 15 |

# Blue whale . . .

The blue whale is the largest animal ever to have lived either on earth or in the sea. It feeds by filtering the surface of the sea, with the comb-like baleen in its mouth, for some of the smallest sea creatures – tiny shrimp-like krill. The sperm whale is the sea's largest and most powerful predator. It has cone-like teeth and dives to great depths to catch its prey.

**The blue whale**
Blue whales over 27m (90 ft) long and weighing up to 100 tons were once common. It takes 11 months for the minute fertilized egg to develop into a calf that might be 7.6m (25 ft) long and weigh up to 3 tons at birth.

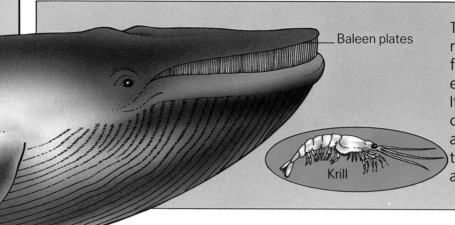

Baleen plates

Krill

The whale feeds by opening its mouth and expanding the folds of its throat to take in an enormous mouthful of water. It then closes its mouth, contracts its throat muscles and squeezes the water through the baleen. The krill are trapped and swallowed.

◁ The photograph shows the enormous tail fluke of a blue whale at the surface. Large numbers have been spotted recently feeding on a huge concentration of krill off California. The North Pacific population of blue whales, perhaps, is beginning to recover. However, in the Southern Ocean there have been few signs of a recovery since the ban on blue whale fishing in 1966. Some researchers believe there are so few that an Antarctic blue whale would have difficulty finding a mate. It is thought that nearly 350,000 have been caught and butchered since the start of the century.

# ...sperm whale

Spermaceti

The sperm whale has a huge bulbous forehead which contains the spermaceti organ, a mass of waxy tissue, used both for buoyancy and for echolocation.

The wax acts like a sound "lens." It focuses very high frequency "click" sounds that are bounced off prey. In this way the whale can locate its prey in the dark depths.

▽ The sperm whale and calf in the photograph below are traveling close to the surface. Occasionally, the adult whale will descend into deeper waters to feed on giant squid, with which it must have enormous battles, and on deep-sea fish. It is thought that the whale is helped to go up and down by changing the density of the wax in its head.

The head becomes heavy when the spermaceti wax, cooled by the surrounding seawater, solidifies. This helps the whale to dive down to more than 1000m (3,300 ft) and remain there for up to 90 minutes. We know sperm whales can dive this deep because they have been tracked by sonar and found caught in undersea cables.

When it wants to return to the surface, warm blood is pumped through the spermaceti. The wax melts and becomes less dense. The head is then more buoyant and this helps the whale to float up – useful if the whale has been chasing squid at great depths and is exhausted. It can reach the surface without much effort.

The sperm whale is a formidable animal. Bulls average 15.25m (50 ft) in length and weigh 36 tons. The largest teeth known are 279mm (11 in) long (from a 27.4m [90 ft] whale). It has the largest known brain, at up to 9.5kg (21 lbs).

# The whalers

The modern whaler stalks his victim in a fast catcher ship, using sonar to follow the whale under the water. The ship follows close to the whale until it begins to slow down. The gunner fires a heavy steel harpoon from a gun in the bow, aiming at a point just behind the whale's head. If the gunner is skilled, the whale dies instantly. If he misses the backbone, the whale might run and writhe, played like a salmon, for up to two hours before it tires and is hauled alongside. Several killer grenades to the head may be required to finish it off. Many whalers have remarked that they would have found it impossible to continue whaling if whales could only cry out or scream.

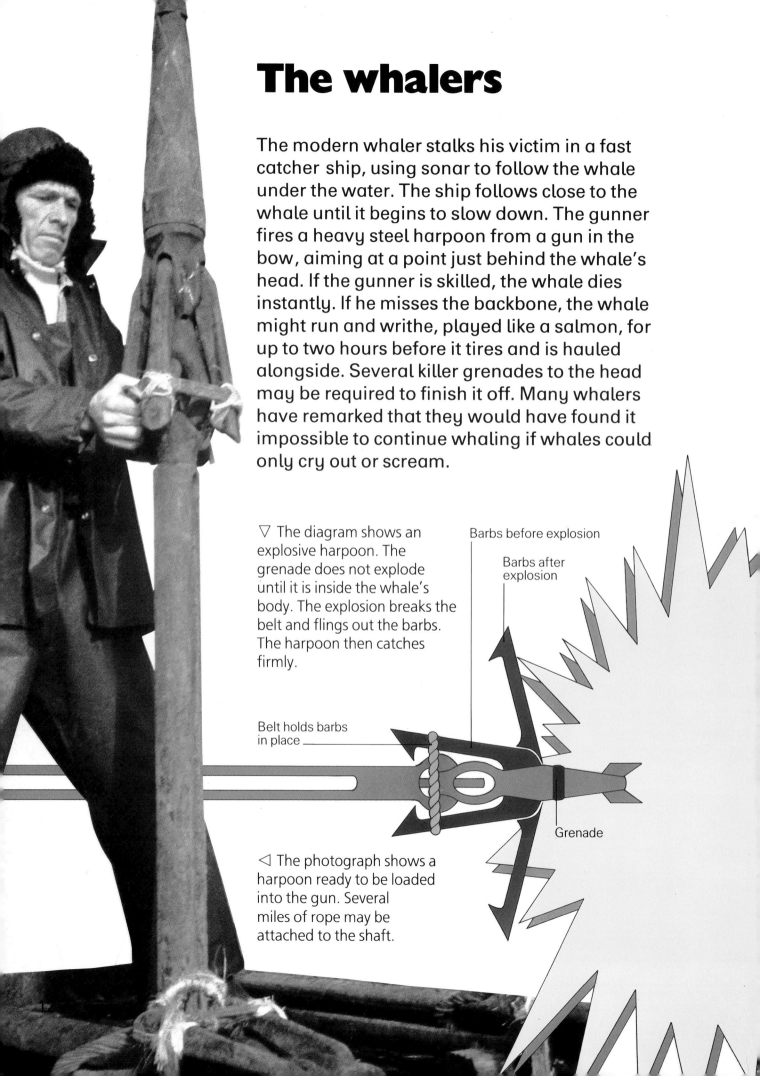

▽ The diagram shows an explosive harpoon. The grenade does not explode until it is inside the whale's body. The explosion breaks the belt and flings out the barbs. The harpoon then catches firmly.

Barbs before explosion

Barbs after explosion

Belt holds barbs in place

Grenade

◁ The photograph shows a harpoon ready to be loaded into the gun. Several miles of rope may be attached to the shaft.

▽ The photograph below shows the moment at which a harpoon hits a great whale. The harpooner will know that the whale is in its final death throes when blood spurts from the blowhole and the sea turns red. The harpooner himself must beware of the line attached to the harpoon. When Svend Foyn, the inventor of the explosive harpoon, first tried it out, the line wrapped around his leg and he ended up in the water alongside the whale!

A catcher boat, working from a factory ship the size of an ocean liner, pumps compressed air into the whale's body so that it floats. A radar reflector, flag or radio beacon is placed on top of the carcass in order that the factory ship, following along behind the catcher boat, can locate the bodies. Sometimes letters from whalers are attached to the whale to be picked up by the factory ship and sent home. On a good day a catcher might take 50 whales.

Fishermen in New Zealand in the 1930s had a very nasty method of catching humpback whales. They were speared with a light harpoon, pumped up with air while still alive, and then a lance with an explosive head was pushed into the body.

"Consider how you would react if you watched someone go into a field and harpoon a cow which then took ten minutes to die."

Sir Peter Scott, one of the founders of the World Wildlife Fund and on the British delegation at the IWC

# The industry

Whaling was once a multi-million dollar industry. As many as 30,000 whales were killed annually during the 1930s, 40s and 50s. Many businessmen became millionaires. There was, however, little thought for the future. The whale industry barons instructed their whalers to catch as many whales as quickly as they could. They did not harvest the whales at a sensible level, but instead they fished out the supply until few whales were left.

Fleets of catcher boats and factory ships would gather up floating whale carcasses for processing. A whale was brought to the stern ramp of the factory ship by a "buoy" boat and hauled by the tail onto a deck the size of a football field. Here, men armed with sharp long-handled "flensing" knives sliced the whale open. Long chunks of blubber were pulled away, much like peeling a banana, by a criss-cross of wire hausers. The rolling deck was covered in slippery blood, blubber and entrails, and holes at the side fed into steam boilers. It was a dangerous place to be. A blue whale would yield about 20-30 tons of oil from the blubber, bones and meat. It was processed in about half an hour. Sometimes, the catchers killed too many whales which would putrify while waiting in the water. Catchers would use them as fenders when coming alongside to take on supplies.

Eventually, great whales became commercially extinct – there were not enough whales left to make the same huge profits – and so the proceeds from the great whaling industry were invested. Whales, it seems, reproduce more slowly than money. Nevertheless, the whaling industry continues today, but on a much smaller scale, as fewer whaling nations attempt to skim off the remaining whales.

The photograph to the right shows a whale factory ship at night. Having been pulled up the stern ramp, whales are first stripped of their blubber on the rear deck (in the background). Then they are pulled to the foredeck where the meat is cut away and the bones sawed into small pieces for boiling. A great whale is being butchered on the foredeck. The workers in the picture below are packing meat from minke whales, one of the smallest of the baleen whales.

# Protection and the IWC

In 1946, there was considerable concern about overfishing in the Antarctic and so the whaling nations formed a "club" called the International Whaling Commission (IWC). It was not concerned at first with conservation but simply with maintaining stocks of whales to be fished. It was not until a ban on whaling was called for at the United Nations Conference on the Environment in Stockholm in 1972 that the IWC emphasis changed to conserving whales.

Unfortunately, the IWC has limited power. Decisions taken to limit catches of rare or endangered species are weakened by nations opting out. The IWC, therefore, can only act as a meeting place for negotiation and debate.

Another problem with the IWC ban is that many nations exploit loopholes in the regulations. These nations continue whaling, justifying it as "aboriginal" – they claim traditional, old-fashioned methods are used. Other nations claim to kill whales for "scientific" purposes, yet still sell the meat to Japan.

△ The photograph shows the IWC in session. Most of the deals between countries are actually done outside the main meeting. A powerful nation can influence a smaller nation, for example, by threatening to pull out of trading agreements or withdrawing fishing rights. Without the IWC, however, matters would clearly be much worse.

"This Commission will be known to history as a small body of men who failed to act responsibly and who protected the interests of a few whalers and not the future of thousands of whales."

The Mexican delegate to the 1974 meeting of the IWC

△ The dead whale in the photograph is a white whale, or beluga. The killing of belugas is part of an "aboriginal" hunt which also involves some of the rarest whales. Many of these so-called aboriginal hunts abuse the IWC ruling. In Alaska, for example, rare bowhead whales are allowed to be taken to satisfy the Inuit (Eskimo) tradition. But, the hunt is carried out from fiberglass boats with outboard motors instead of sealskin kayaks, using rifles instead of bone-tipped spears.

# The Faeroes *grind*

Each year, for the past four centuries, the people of the Faeroes (a group of Danish islands lying between Iceland and Britain) have driven the *grindvhal* – pilot whales – toward the shore and slaughtered them. Pilot whale meat and blubber once helped these islanders to survive. The hunt itself brought isolated communities together; it was a festival.

The pilot whale hunt is now the largest kill of any whale species in the northern hemisphere. Up to 2,500 whales are butchered each year and since 1709 nearly a quarter of a million whales have been killed. The hunt is outside the IWC's ruling so there is no limit to the numbers.

▽ The photograph shows a pilot whale kill. Traditionally, rowboats were used and stones were thrown in the water to frighten the whales back onto the beach where they were killed quickly. A long knife severed the spinal column just behind the head. Today, motorboats and loud airhorns stampede the whales. Unskilled hunters attempt to kill the whales in the water. The whales swim in their own blood.

Today, the export of fish has made the Faeroese relatively wealthy people. They have a standard of living comparable to any Scandinavian country. They do not need the pilot whale meat. Indeed, not all of the whale carcass is used. After choice parts have been removed, the bones, head and guts are towed out to sea. The liver and kidneys are contaminated with mercury and cannot be eaten. Old meat is sometimes discarded on garbage dumps and replaced by new in freezers. Curiously, the Faeroese have been taking the largest numbers of whales in recent years. Some observers consider the *grind* to be a sport rather than an aboriginal kill.

▷ The Faeroese child in the photograph is playing with a pilot whale fetus. The boy is too young to join in the hunt and the killing, which may take up to five hours to complete. The meat is shared by every person taking part in the hunt and often the number of whales exceeds the demand for meat. After a kill in 1981, for example, 300 dead whales were left untouched.

# Action!

◁ The photograph shows Greenpeace supporters in an inflatable boat. They are harassing a Russian whale catcher. Protesters often attempt to put themselves between the whale and the harpoon gun. They hope that the gunner will be prevented from firing. By disturbing whaling in this way, they draw attention to the killing and save at least a few whales from being slaughtered.

▽ Anti-whaling supporters, like those in this photograph, also use more peaceful means of protest. Demonstrations outside the embassies of pro-whaling nations, petitions and public meetings draw people's attention to the plight of whales and attract further support for the cause.

Each June, the plight of the whales is front page news, as this is the time of the annual meeting of the IWC. But how is whaling kept in the news for the rest of the year?

Many people believe that it takes direct action by the environmental pressure groups, such as Greenpeace, to prick the world's conscience. By placing themselves in dangerous situations – harassing whaling fleets on the high seas, for instance – they attract the attention of the world's press. This ensures that news of whales and whaling reaches those people who otherwise would not know or care.

Other organizations, such as Sea Shepherd, have gone further and sunk whale catchers and wrecked shore stations. Some think they have helped create public opinion against whaling and therefore have brought pressure to bear on the politicians who negotiate whaling matters at the IWC. Others, however, believe that their commando-style operations do harm to whales because they anger the pro-whaling nations and consequently delay any conservation agreements.

SAVE THE WHALES
BEGIN TO SAVE THE WORLD

# The plight of the dolphins

Dolphins are small toothed whales. It is often overlooked that they too are killed. In the 1970s, the Turkish dolphin fishing-ground in the Black Sea accounted for the killing of 176,000 dolphins a year. In 1980 the catch had dropped to 75,000. In 1981 only 25,000 were caught. The population had crashed, probably due to overfishing.

Despite a government ban, the dolphins are still caught on their annual migrations. Each winter, hunters all along the Black Sea coast of Turkey reach for their rifles and harpoons. The dolphins are killed illegally to provide oil from the blubber and animal food from the minced-up meat and bones.

"Dolphins are very smart. They can tell the sounds of our engines from those of regular fishing boats. But we still kill about one out of eight."

Ahmet Com
Turkish Black Sea
dolphin hunter

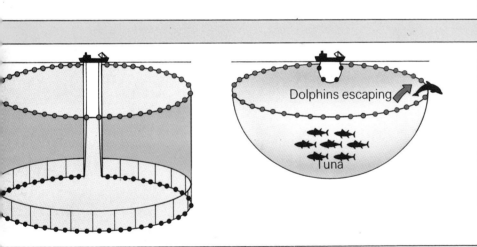

Dolphins escaping

Tuna

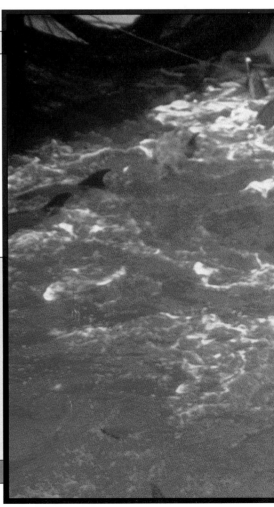

△ The purse-seine net in the diagram is one of the most efficient ways of catching fish. When the net is closed, nothing can escape. In the Pacific the target fish are yellowfin tuna. But swimming with them are dolphins, so the dolphins are trapped too.

Purse-seine nets today must have a special panel through which the dolphin can escape without releasing the fish. Each tuna boat also carries a diver who helps the dolphins to find their way out of the net. In this way at least some dolphins are saved.

During the past two decades, a million dolphins have been slaughtered. Yet the greatest number of deaths are accidental. About 10,000 Dall's porpoises die each year entangled in discarded fishing gear. In the eastern Pacific, dolphins swimming with yellowfin tuna are caught in the nets of the tuna fishermen. In 1974, over 500,000 dolphins died in tuna nets. Today, US tuna boats must have special nets that allow the dolphins to escape. Boats have scuba divers on board to help the animals get out. Nevertheless, 40,000 a year still die. Since tuna fishermen first started using nets, about five million dolphins have been killed.

▽ The photograph shows Japanese fishermen killing hundreds of dolphins. The dolphins are killed because both dolphins and fishermen compete for the same fish stocks. The Japanese Fisheries Agency tried to find ways of frightening the dolphins away. A model killer whale was placed in the water which emitted calls to scare off the dolphins, but they simply played with it! There are no plans to stop the slaughter.

# Narwhals and dolphins

All the small whales and dolphins are toothed whales which hunt fish and squid. Many have a bulbous forehead which contains a mass of fatty tissue that focuses high frequency sounds for echolocation. The sounds are so powerful that some researchers think that dolphins not only "see" their prey with sound, but also harm it or even kill it with the high frequency sound. Calves are born at sea and are helped to the surface to take their first breath. As whales are mammals, the young suckle.

### The narwhal
Male narwhals may be 5m (16 ft) in body length and have tusks 3m (10 ft) long. Females are up to 4m (13 ft) long and calves are 1.5m (5 ft) at birth. They eat mainly Arctic cod, shrimp and flatfish. The tusk is sometimes used to flush out flounders from the sea bed.

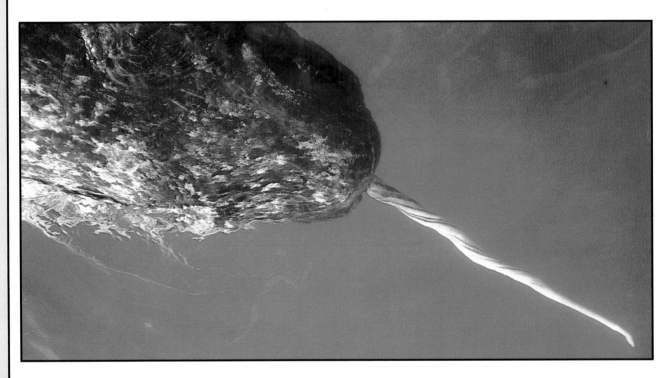

△ The narwhal in the photograph is a male. It uses its tusk for sword duels with other males. The animal is known as the "unicorn of the seas." The tusk, which is spiraled, is not a horn but an elongated tooth in the upper left jaw. Females and juvenile males do not have a tusk.

The tusk is a valuable collectors' item, but restrictions on trade in whale products have meant the market for new tusks is often an illegal one. Nevertheless, a tusk may change hands for over $5,000. In the past it was thought to be magical and an antidote to poisons.

Narwhals live in the Arctic. They are often found swimming with belugas or white whales. Although there are hunting restrictions on narwhals, it is thought that they are possibly being hunted faster than they can reproduce. They are shot when they break the surface to take air.

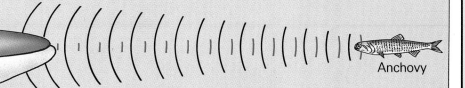
Anchovy

Bottlenose dolphin

The diagram shows how the dolphin's sound beam travels through the water, bounces off an object such as an anchovy, and returns.

The sound is produced in the head, focused in the forehead and the echo is received by the lower jaw. The powerful beam can stun or kill prey.

**The dolphin**
Dolphins can swim in bursts at speeds of up to 20mph and jump 18 ft into the air. The largest dolphin is the killer whale, or orca, with a length of 24 ft, and one of the smallest is the harbor porpoise at 5 ft.

△ The photograph shows a school of Pacific bottlenose dolphins "porpoising" in the water. It has been shown that shallow swimming and leaping is the most efficient way a dolphin can travel. This is aided by the dolphin's streamlined torpedo-shaped body and powerful tail muscles.

Dolphins tend to travel in schools. Sometimes as many as 2,000 may be moving together. When hunting, subgroups of 20 or 30 animals might swim in line abreast, communicating with squeaks and burps. They scan the broad area of sea ahead with their echolocation beams.

Dolphins have large brains. They are considered to be intelligent animals, perhaps with a sophisticated language for communication. Currently, several scientific research programs are underway in an attempt to unravel their language and to talk directly to them.

# Whales and dolphins in captivity

Dolphins, killer whales, belugas and pilot whales have performed in aquariums and marine circuses since the first was built in Florida in 1938. Today, performing dolphins are big business. A killer whale may be sold for $500,000.

But there is a serious moral dilemma here. Most captive dolphins have been caught and brought in from the wild. There are few births in aquariums; in fact, there have been no more than 200. In addition, dolphins and killer whales, deprived of their freedom, do not live long. This fact is often disguised; when a killer whale dies it is quickly replaced and its successor given the same name.

Pilot whales and dolphins are also kept in captivity to help in military and scientific experiments. They have been trained to recover torpedoes from the bottom of the sea, to attach explosives to enemy ships, to detect submarines and to guard harbor entrances.

▷ The dolphins and killer whale in the photograph would not be found together in the wild. Killer whales may eat dolphins. In captivity, the stress of peformances and fights for dominance may give them gastric ulcers, just like humans. Conservationists are concerned. They question whether these animals should be kept in captivity to entertain and educate the public. Many believe they should be left to live their lives in the wild.

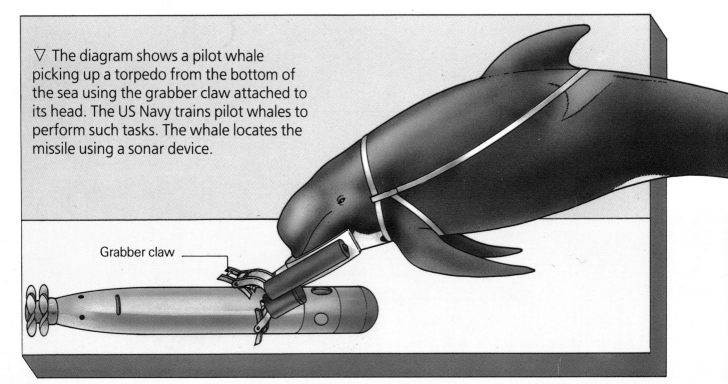

▽ The diagram shows a pilot whale picking up a torpedo from the bottom of the sea using the grabber claw attached to its head. The US Navy trains pilot whales to perform such tasks. The whale locates the missile using a sonar device.

Grabber claw

"The keeping of whales and dolphins in captivity will always pose problems because of the contradiction on which it is based: the keeping in cramped conditions of creatures which are accustomed to vast open spaces."

Professor George Pilleri, University of Berne, Switzerland

"If we can't save the whale, we can't save anything, including the human species. Whales are a symbol of survival, and perhaps the symbol of all conservation."

Sir Peter Scott, one of the founder members of the World Wildlife Fund

# The future

◁ This photograph shows two fully grown southern right whales and a calf at the Peninsula Valdes in Argentina. Both the northern and southern races of right whales suffered from intensive whaling in the 19th century. Populations are slowly recovering but it is estimated that there are still only about 2,000 throughout the world's oceans.

▽ The baby gray whale in this photograph has a radio transmitter attached to its back. This allows scientists to follow the whale on its annual migrations along the Pacific coast of North America. They can monitor the whale's autumn journey to its breeding grounds at Baja California and its return in summer to the feeding grounds in Alaska.

How safe are the whales? Will the present ban on commercial whaling be extended indefinitely, or will the pro-whaling nations once more return to whaling? If nations cannot agree about the future of whaling, might organizations like the IWC be in danger of breaking up? Could there then be a "free-for-all" to catch whales? And are there enough whales to catch commercially without threatening them with extinction?

The key factor in all these questions is how many whales remain. Whales are extremely difficult to count as they spend much of their lives under sea. Ways have been devised, from recognizing whales by their markings to tracking them by satellite. But there is, at present, no way of knowing the state of whale stocks.

But should we catch whales anyway? Or should these intelligent and gentle creatures be given a new status? There have been suggestions that whale catchers be turned into whale watchers to create a very different kind of industry! Are we going to save the whales or will the human race be responsible for the annihilation of the greatest creatures to have lived on earth?

# Whale facts

*The blue areas on the maps show whale distribution*

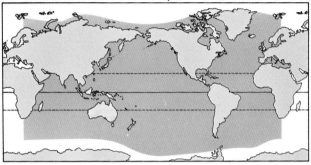

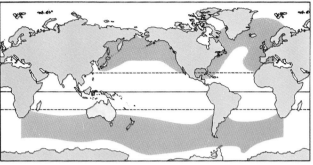

### Blue, fin, sei and minke whales

The blue, fin, sei and minke whales are found in seas all around the world. During the summer they tend to move toward polar seas where they feed intensively on the dense swarms of fish and plankton. Exactly where they go in the winter is a mystery, but they certainly move toward warmer waters in order to breed and are thought to eat very little for several months.

### Right whales

The northern and the southern right whales breed in shallow bays and feed in coastal waters. Surprisingly, a breeding bay for northern right whales in the North Atlantic was discovered only recently on the east coast of the United States, off the coast of Georgia. Historically, their predictable coastal habits resulted in them being easy prey for whalers.

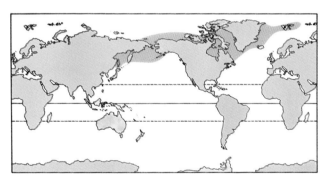

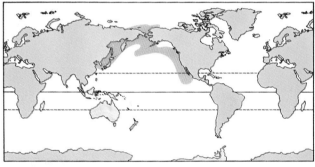

### Bowhead whales

Like the right whales, bowheads are rare. The total world population is only about 3,500. They prefer coastal waters but venture out to sea by following the edge of the Arctic pack-ice. If trapped, they can burst through thick ice in order to make a hole to breathe. Bowheads are still hunted by Inuit (Eskimos) along the coast of Alaska where they are pulled up onto the ice after being killed.

### Gray whales

In September gray whales leave the Bering, Chukchi and Okhotsk seas and head south to breed. The eastern Pacific whales go to Baja California and the western ones go to Korea. In the spring they return to the Arctic to feed. This species is unique in that it feeds by filtering small organisms from the mud on the sea bed. As a result, it doesn't have the throat grooves needed by most other baleen whales to feed.

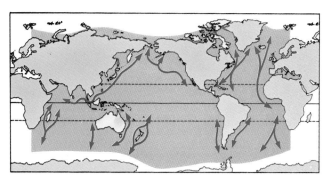

## Humpback whales

Humpbacks in the southern hemisphere breed in the Mozambique Channel and off Australia, New Hebrides, Fiji, Ecuador and Brazil. The northern whales breed off Hawaii, Baja (Mexico), West Indies and the Cape Verde Islands. They migrate along well-known coastal routes (indicated by the arrows) to feed in polar seas.

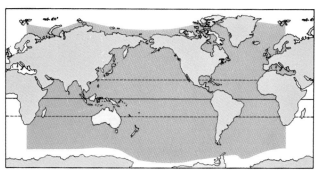

## Sperm whales

Sperm whales are found in all oceans, particularly at the edges of deep trenches. The cows and family groups tend to spend most time in the tropics, although there is a move to temperate waters in summer. Most bulls migrate even farther, toward the polar seas. Bulls are usually found singly or in small groups of 10 to 40.

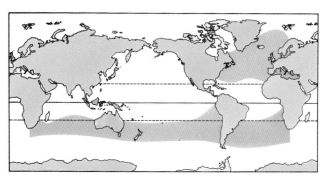

## Longfin pilot whales

Longfin pilot whales prefer cool, deep waters. If they encounter shallows on their migrations they are likely to become stranded. It is not clear how many longfin pilot whales remain. They can be easily confused with tropical shortfin whales. The populations of the two species probably overlap. Although originally from one stock, northern and southern hemisphere whales now look quite different.

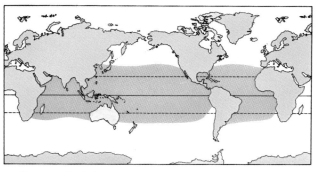

## Spinner dolphins

Spinner dolphins live in tropical waters, often in association with spotted and bridled dolphins and tuna. The population most often caught by tuna fishermen in the tropical eastern Pacific is thought to number more than three million dolphins. Research in most parts of the world has shown that some dolphins have an inshore and an offshore form which rarely overlap.

# Index

**Photographic Credits:**
Cover: Philip Allen/Planet Earth; pages 4-5, 28
and back cover: Survival Anglia; pages 6 (left),
12, 13 and 15 (top): Nigel Merret/Planet Earth;
page 6 (right), 15 (bottom), 18, 19 and 21:
Dave Currey/Environmental Investigation
Agency; pages 8, 10, 11, 25 and 29: Bruce
Colman; page 16: International Whaling
Commission; pages 17 and 24: Brian and
Cherry Alexander; page 20 and 22-23:
Greenpeace; page 27: Syndication
International.

PRINTED IN BELGIUM BY
proost
INTERNATIONAL BOOK PRODUCTION